TRUMPITUDE

TRUMPITUDE

THE SECRET CONFESSIONS OF DONALD'S BRAIN

ALSO AVAILABLE IN
RUSSIAN!

ELLIS HENICAN
ART BY RANDY JONES

A POST HILL PRESS BOOK
ISBN: 978-1-68261-510-2
ISBN (eBook): 978-1-68261-511-9

Trumpitude:
The Secret Confessions of Donald's Brain
© 2017 by Ellis Henican
All Rights Reserved

Art by Randy Jones

Post Hill Press
New York · Nashville
posthillpress.com

Published in the United States of America

Table of Contents

Sleep is for sissies.

Big, Beautiful Gobs of Trumpitude

Are you tired of winning yet? Donald Trump warned this could be a problem once the gold-colored drapes were installed in the Oval Office and America got suddenly great again.

"You're gonna be so sick and tired of winning," Trump roared to the rally faithful over and over again. "You'll say, 'Please, please, Mister President. It's too much winning. We can't take it anymore.'"

No one's complained about *that* lately.

Quite the opposite, in fact.

But that quote, right there, is a perfect manifestation of something that I have begun calling Trumpitude, the constantly-swirling mix of swagger, self-delusion, and straight-faced lies that comprise the very essence of America's 45th president.

Trumpitude.

Not party or ideology. Not policy or plan.

Pure, combustible Trumpitude.

Please step lightly! Any second, it could blow!

* * *

We know what Trump says to the Fox News anchors. We know how he thunders to the star-struck rally crowds. We know how he loves to tweet at 5 a.m. He is saying things. They are words. *Huuuuge! Cheye-nah! Co-luuuude!* But none of it quite makes sense. The assertions are objectively groundless. The assumptions are downright bizarre. The sputtering claims? They are mostly untethered from reality. (*Obama tapped Trump Tower.... Massive voter fraud.... Greatest election victory since Reagan.... Highest murder rate in 47 years... Comey was too mean to Hillary Clinton... No campaign aides ever met with Russians... Deporting only "bad hombres."*) And when the inevitable defenses have to be raised, they too are constructed from thin air. ("I have articles saying it happened." *Ohhh-kay!*) The scary question is how much of this drivel the president actually believes, how the inside of his brain is connected, if at all, to what just came flying off his tongue. But this much is certain: Every last syllable is slathered with gobs of Trumpitude.

A lot has happened since the narcissistic New Yorker took the oath of office in front of a so-so crowd on the Washington mall—*the largest crowd ever!*—and a grim reality set in.

"Drain the swamp" turned into a white-flag surrender. "Ban the Muslims" got hog-tied in court. "Build the wall" became a punchline almost as preposterous as "make Mexico pay." "Repeal and replace" became "repeal and oh-never-mind." Russia became an official election swing state. Tax reform, infrastructure, the end of terror as we knew it, a post-NATO Europe, an America-first world—whatever the promises were, they went down as fast as the president's approval rating and almost as far.

Suddenly, the only one who was smiling was Vladimir Putin. Even a certain 400-pound American computer genius looked confused. "Wasn't hacking the election supposed to *my* job?" he asked, sitting in his mama's basement on an unmade bed.

Sorry, Basement Boy! Vladimir's dropping by the White House, and he'll be riding horses shirtless in the Rose Garden!

* * *

How does Donald Trump do it—whatever *it* is? Can anyone stop him now? What does he know that the rest of us haven't caught onto? Isn't it time we all found out?

You bet it is.

But you won't find answers in the White House briefing room or even in the "fake-news" media. That's what this little book is for. It's a cheat sheet to the inside of the president's brain. It reveals what Donald Trump is really thinking, whether he knows it or not. It is packed with his own advice on how to be more Trumpian. Through the power of insight and analysis— and some well-placed logical leaps—*Trumpitude* reveals the many twists and turns of, you guessed it, Trumpitude.

To understand Trump, sometimes you have to think like him. To answer Trump, sometimes you have to talk like him. To combat Trump, you don't need a degree from Trump University. You don't have to embrace his upside-down world view— how could you? But you do need to remember that China is our enemy—no, China is our friend—no, they're our enemy— no, they're our friend. You get the idea!

Having covered Trump from his boy-developer days in New York City, I know better than anyone that the regular rules do not apply. But other rules can and do. We just need to grasp them.

He'll lie to you for no good reason. He'll flatter you and then insult you and forget he did either one. That can leave your head spinning, but it also has its benefits. I can now chart Trump's every personality quirk and mental *cul-de-sac*—and still come out the other side. I know that a sufficient application of hairspray can suspend the normal force of gravity.

It's Trump's America now. We just live here. But we'd damn well better understand what's happening. We need to identify the Trumpitude correctly. Once we do that, we can hurl it like a boomerang right back at him.

Since Donald Trump does not operate by words alone, neither can we. I have recruited one of America's finest artists and illustrators, Randy Jones, to explore some of these concepts in his own twistedly brilliant way. When words begin to fail us, Randy and his pencils step valiantly in.

When it comes to this force called Trumpitude, everything is here.

The Great Moments and Lessons Learned: How the facts of Donald's journey, like a dusty attic packed with seven decades of junk, helped to forge a future president. Rustle around in there— you never know what you might find.

The Trump-to-English Translator: Vital for anyone who wants to understand the president's often-murky meanings.

Finish Donald's Thought: This isn't fair, but it's necessary. It puts the onus on the ruled to amplify the ruler. It leads down some spooky paths.

All that, plus Donald's Delusional Definitions, his 24-Carat Golden Rules (no 16-carat for him) and some bonus sidebars and puzzlers that explore his love of nicknames, his dreams of

Hollywood, his appeal to rappers and a bunch of other please-I-gotta-go rest stops on the road to Trumpitude.

Yes, it's a long, strange journey we are on now. But the scenery is certainly striking. I promise, the destination isn't that far off. And really, what choice do we have as proud and patriotic Americans? Isn't the future of our nation at stake?

Major Moments,
Lessons Learned

MAJOR MOMENT: June 14, 1946

Donald John Trump is born at Jamaica Hospital in Queens,
New York, the fourth child of Fred and Mary Trump.
Little Donny is welcomed at his family's 23-room mansion on
Midland Parkway in the posh Jamaica Estates neighborhood.

LESSON LEARNED

Why be poor? Rich is way nicer.

MAJOR MOMENT: 1952

As a precocious 5-year-old, Donald follows his babysitter
into a sewer under construction in the neighborhood.
Despite the darkness, the boy does not panic or cry.

LESSON LEARNED

Life's an adventure,
even if you are totally in the dark.

SPELL WITH TRUMPITUDE

The Tweeter-in-Chief keeps using his executive power to invent words.

Chocker (for shocker)

Dummer (for dumber)

Hearby (for hereby)

Honered (for honored)

Insticts (for instincts)

Leightweight (for lightweight)

Phoneix (for Phoenix)

Rediculous (for ridiculous)

Shoker (for shocker)

Tapp (for tap)

Unpresidented (for unprecedented)

Covfefe (nobody has any idea what that is!)

MAJOR MOMENT: 1953

At the private Kew-Forest School, young Donald may or may not have socked his second-grade music teacher in the face, giving the man a black eye. Though the story is vividly recounted in *Trump: The Art of the Deal*, it is later denied by the teacher and the Kew-Forest classmates.

LESSON LEARNED

Fake news is fun.

If you have ugly friends, you'll always be
the best looking guy in the room.

MAJOR MOMENT: September 1959

After Donald's parents catch him sneaking into Manhattan without permission, they ship him off to boarding school at New York Military Academy.

LESSON LEARNED

Military school isn't so bad.
They let you order the little kids around.

MAJOR MOMENT: August 1964

The University of Southern California says
thanks but no thanks to Donald's application,
sidetracking his dream of being a Hollywood producer.
Instead, the New York Military Academy grad attends
Fordham University, the one college that accepts him.

LESSON LEARNED

There is more than one path into showbiz.

HOLLYWOOD TRUMPITUDE

"Meryl Streep, one of the most overrated actresses in Hollywood..."

It's Donald Trump's star-studded truth: No one has more star power than he does. Too bad Hollywood doesn't agree. Can you pick the real stars of these "Trump movies"? They all got higher billing than Trump did.

1. *Eddie* (1996)
2. *Ghosts Can't Do It* (1989)
3. *Home Alone 2: Lost in New York* (1992)
4. *The Associate* (1996)
5. *The Little Rascals* (1994)
6. *Two Weeks Notice* (2002)
7. *Zoolander* (2001)

A. Ben Stiller, Owen Wilson
B. Bo Derek, Anthony Quinn
C. Macaulay Culkin, Joe Pesci
D. Petey the Dog
E. Sandra Bullock, Hugh Grant
F. Whoopi Goldberg, Dianne Wiest
G. Whoopi Goldberg, Frank Langella

BONUS QUESTION

Razzie Awards are presented each year in recognition of the very worst in film. Which Trumpitudinous performance earned Donald the Razzie for Worst Supporting Actor?

HOLLYWOOD TRUMPITUDE
CORRECT ANSWERS

1. *Eddie* (1996)
2. *Ghosts Can't Do It* (1989)
3. *Home Alone 2: Lost in New York* (1992)
4. *The Associate* (1996)
5. *The Little Rascals* (1994)
6. *Two Weeks Notice* (2002)
7. *Zoolander* (2001)

G. Whoopi Goldberg, Frank Langella
B. Bo Derek, Anthony Quinn
C. Macaulay Culkin, Joe Pesci
F. Whoopi Goldberg, Dianne Wiest
D. Petey the Dog
E. Sandra Bullock, Hugh Grant
A. Ben Stiller, Owen Wilson

BONUS ANSWER: Donald Trump won the Worst Supporting Actor Razzie for his appearance in *Ghosts Can't Do It*.

MAJOR MOMENT: June 1968

A third-year transfer student, Donald graduates
from the Wharton School at the University of Pennsylvania
with a degree in real-estate studies. He takes a job with his
father's real-estate development firm.

LESSON LEARNED

Attend a college where your father is a major donor.
Major in your father's field.

MAJOR MOMENT: February 1, 1972

After four student and medical deferments,
Donald is declared ineligible for military service
in the Vietnam War.

LESSON LEARNED

Other people can do the fighting. Let them.

MAJOR MOMENT: October 6, 1973

U.S. Justice Department accuses the Trump Organization of discriminating against black homebuyers, a violation of the Fair Housing Act. Admitting no wrong-doing, the company reaches a settlement.

LESSON LEARNED

Dispute what you have to, settle what you can't.

Deny everything. Then deny
that you denied it.

MAJOR MOMENT: April 7, 1977

Donald marries Czechoslovakian skier
and aspiring model Ivana Zelníčková.

LESSON LEARNED

Not all immigrants should be banned from America—
certainly not the ones who are tall and blond
and have cute accents.

MAJOR MOMENT: December 31, 1977

Donald John Trump Jr. is born, followed by Ivanka Marie Trump
(October 30, 1981) and Eric Frederick Trump (January 6, 1984).
Busy at work, their father leaves most of the
childrearing to his wife.

LESSON LEARNED

Women are better at some things than men.

At the White House, every day is 'bring your kids to work' day.

MAJOR MOMENT: 1980

Building on his father's successes in Brooklyn and Queens,
young Donald renovates the old Commodore Hotel at
Grand Central Terminal into the shiny Grand Hyatt.
New York tabloids agree: He's arrived.

LESSON LEARNED

Outer boroughs are boring. Manhattan's where it's at.

MAJOR MOMENT: July 27, 1982

Mayor Ed Koch joins Donald Trump on Fifth Avenue for the opening of Trump Tower, despite claims that off-the-books Polish workers were hired during construction.

LESSON LEARNED

In real estate and politics, there is no penalty for saying one thing and doing another. Yay hypocrisy!

Nothing glitters like my name on stuff.

MAJOR MOMENT: 1991

For the first of four times, a Trump company seeks protection
from Chapter 11 of the U.S. Bankruptcy Law.
He retains control of his three Atlantic City casinos
and posh Plaza Hotel, but is forced to unload the Trump Shuttle
and his 282-foot Trump Princess yacht.

LESSON LEARNED

Bankruptcy is the government's way of saying,
"Don't worry, it's okay that you failed."

MAJOR MOMENT: December 20, 1993

After divorcing his wife Ivana, Donald marries actress
and fitness buff Marla Maples,
mother of two-month-old Tiffany Trump.

LESSON LEARNED

Don't be a stickler for the old-fashioned order of things.

Always comment on your daughter's figure. That doesn't sound creepy at all.

MAJOR MOMENT: October 24, 1996

Trump buys Miss Universe, Miss USA
and Miss Teen pageants from ITT Corp.

LESSON LEARNED

Beauty contestants are way prettier
than construction workers.

MAJOR MOMENT: January 8, 2004

The Apprentice premieres on NBC.

LESSON LEARNED

Playing a successful businessman on television
is easier than being a successful businessman.

How I'm approaching my
amazing presidency.

MAJOR MOMENT: October 1, 2004

Donald J. Trump Signature Collection
including fat, red neckties arrives in department stores.

LESSON LEARNED

Shoppers will buy anything at all
with a celebrity's name on it.

Slap your name on everything you can—
except the signature line of a check.

BRAND WITH TRUMPITUDE

When you have a winning name, why hide it?
Go ahead! Slap it on just about everything! See if you
can spot the 5 items Trump HASN'T branded...YET!

Trump Barstools
Trump Bedding
Trump Beer
Trump Board Game
Trump Cabinets
Trump Chandeliers
Trump Cologne
Trump Cufflinks
Trump Deodorant
Trump Dress Shirts
Trump Eyeglasses
Trump Hair Products
Trump Hand Sanitizer
Trump Lamps
Trump Magazine

Trump Mirrors
Trump Mortgages
Trump Natural Spring
    Water
Trump Neckties
Trump Rifles
Trump Shuttle
Trump Steaks
Trump Suits
Trump University
Trump Vodka
Trump Wallets
Trump Wedding Dresses
Trump Wine

BRAND WITH TRUMPITUDE
CORRECT ANSWERS

Donald Trump has boasted that his brand name is worth over
3 billion dollars. No one knows if that is true. What we do know
is that the Trump name appears on thousands and thousands of
products.

But, incredibly, not these...not yet.

Beer
Hair Products
Hand Sanitizer
Rifles
Wedding Dresses

MAJOR MOMENT: January 22, 2005

Donald marries Slovenian supermodel
Melania Knauss.

LESSON LEARNED

If a model is good, a supermodel must be even better.

Choose a wife who speaks enough English to follow orders but not so much that she expresses opinions of her own.

MAJOR MOMENT: 2005

With *Access Hollywood* host Billy Bush egging him on,
the newly-married Trump is caught on a hot mic
bragging about sexually assaulting women,
a recording that stays secret for 11 years.

LESSON LEARNED

None.

Women should be grabbed
and not heard.

MAJOR MOMENT: May 23, 2005

Classes begin at Trump University. "I can turn anyone into a successful real-estate investor, including you," 93-percent owner Donald Trump declares.

LESSON LEARNED

A sucker is born every minute, which, ironically, is also lesson number one at Trump University.

MAJOR MOMENT: March 20, 2006

Barron William Trump is born.

LESSON LEARNED

Barron? That makes Dad a king, right?

MAJOR MOMENT: October 24, 2012

Donald Trump offers $5 million to charity if Barack Obama
releases his birth certificate.
Later, he increases the offer to $50 million.

LESSON LEARNED

There's a difference between "offering" and "spending."
Offer, don't spend.

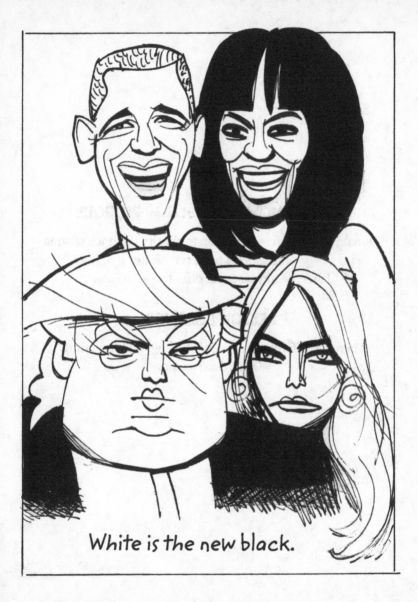

White is the new black.

MAJOR MOMENT: June 16, 2015

Donald Trump rides the down escalator at Trump Tower,
then quickly calls Mexican immigrants
"rapists" and drug dealers.

LESSON LEARNED

In America, anyone can grow up to be president.

Pray for your president—and to him.

TRUMP-TO-ENGLISH TRANSLATOR

Trump-to-English Translator

TRUMP

"After I win, I will be so presidential that you won't even recognize me. You'll be falling asleep, you'll be so bored."

—*WASHINGTON POST* INTERVIEW

ENGLISH

Don't worry, President Trump will be the same narcissistic attention hog as Candidate Trump. I'm too old to change!

Trump-to-English Translator

TRUMP

"Nobody respects women more than Donald Trump."

—RALLY IN EUGENE, OREGON

ENGLISH

Nobody REJECTS women more than Donald Trump.

Go on The Howard Stern Show every
chance you get. Howard will never let
you say anything embarassing.

Trump-to-English Translator

TRUMP

"President Xi, we have a, like, a really great relationship."
—ASSOCIATED PRESS INTERVIEW

ENGLISH

*I'm sure the Chinese president has completely forgotten
I called him a currency manipulator,
an illegal dumper, an intellectual-property thief,
and North Korea's sugar tit.*

THE TRUMPITUDINOUS GUEST

Before Trump commanded the *Apprentice* boardroom, he added Trumpitude to lots of other TV shows. Still, despite his obvious availability, some programs decided a Donald cameo wasn't quite the right fit. Which are the REAL appearances and which are FAKE?

1.	*Cheers*	Real or Fake
2.	*Days of Our Lives*	Real or Fake
3.	*General Hospital*	Real or Fake
4.	*Golden Girls*	Real or Fake
5.	*Hart to Hart*	Real or Fake
6.	*I'll Take Manhattan*	Real or Fake
7.	*King of Queens*	Real or Fake
8.	*Married with Children*	Real or Fake
9.	*Sex and the City*	Real or Fake
10.	*Spin City*	Real or Fake
11.	*Suddenly Susan*	Real or Fake
12.	*The Drew Carey Show*	Real or Fake
13.	*The Fresh Prince of Bel-Air*	Real or Fake
14.	*The Jeffersons*	Real or Fake
15.	*The Job*	Real or Fake
16.	*The Nanny*	Real or Fake
17.	*Who's the Boss?*	Real or Fake

THE TRUMPITUDINOUS GUEST
CORRECT ANSWERS

Real

2. *Days of Our Lives*
5. *Hart to Hart*
6. *I'll Take Manhattan*
9. *Sex and the City*
10. *Spin City*
11. *Suddenly Susan*
12. *The Drew Carey Show*
13. *The Fresh Prince of Bel-Air*
14. *The Jeffersons*
15. *The Job*
16. *The Nanny*

Fake

1. *Cheers*
3. *General Hospital*
4. *Golden Girls*
7. *King of Queens*
8. *Married with Children*
14. *The Jeffersons*
17. *Who's the Boss?*

Trump-to-English Translator

TRUMP

"I have great relationships with Congress."

—ASSOCIATED PRESS INTERVIEW

ENGLISH

I ask Congress for something. They don't do it.
Then I ask them for something else.
Oh, we work together beautifully.

Trump-to-English Translator

TRUMP

"You're going to end up with great health care
for a fraction of the price and that's gonna take place
immediately after we go in.
Okay? Immediately. Fast. Quick."

–Rally in Las Vegas, Nevada

ENGLISH

Just don't get sick. Okay?

Trump-to-English Translator

TRUMP

"I'm afraid the election's going to be rigged,
I have to be honest."

–Rally in Columbus, Ohio

ENGLISH

*I'm afraid the election's going to be rigged,
I have to be honest—rigged for me.
If not, Putin's got some 'splaining to do.*

Trump-to-English Translator

TRUMP

"Russia, if you're listening, I hope you're able to find
the 30,000 emails that are missing.
I think you will probably be rewarded mightily by our press."

—Campaign press conference in Doral, Florida

ENGLISH

Let's collude! Give Don Jr. a call.

Trump-to-English Translator

TRUMP

"When the audit is complete, I will release them."

—Campaign press conference in Doral, Florida

ENGLISH

When the audit is complete, I still won't release them.
I will never, ever, ever, ever, no matter what, release my taxes.
Do you have any idea what I admit to in there?

COVERED WITH TRUMPITUDE

"I have been on their cover, like, 14 or 15 times. I think
we have the all-time record in the history of *Time*
magazine." But which of these fine magazines have
NEVER chosen Donald Trump as cover boy?

1. *American Cowboy*
2. *Bella*
3. *Bon Appétit*
4. *Car and Driver*
5. *Der Spiegel*
6. *ESPN*
7. *Esquire*
8. *Forbes*
9. *Fortune*
10. *Glamour*
11. *Golf Digest*
12. *GQ*
13. *Le Point*
14. *Mad*
15. *Maxim*
16. *New York*
17. *Newsweek*
18. *Parenting*
19. *People*
20. *Playboy*
21. *Popular Science*
22. *Rolling Stone*
23. *Russian Life*
24. *Spy*
25. *Star*
26. *The Atlantic*
27. *The Hollywood Reporter*
28. *Trump Magazine*
29. *TV Guide*
30. *Vanity Fair*
31. *Variety*
32. *Wedding Style*

COVERED WITH TRUMPITUDE
CORRECT ANSWERS

"Do I look like a president? How handsome am I, right? How handsome?" Not handsome enough to make these covers.

1. *American Cowboy*
3. *Bon Appetit*
4. *Car and Driver*
6. *ESPN*
10. *Glamour*
15. *Maxim*

18. *Parenting*
21. *Popular Science*
23. *Russian Life*
25. *Star*
29. *TV Guide*
32. *Wedding Style*

Trump-to-English Translator

"I alone can fix it."
–At Republican National Convention

ENGLISH

I alone can't fix it, whatever IT is.

Trump-to-English Translator

"But you also had people that were very fine people,
on both sides."

–PRESS CONFERENCE AT TRUMP TOWER, NEW YORK CITY

ENGLISH

Some of my best friends are neo-Nazis and Klansmen.

Trump-to-English Translator

TRUMP

"The only one that cares about my tax returns
are the reporters."

–Post-election press conference

ENGLISH

*Reporters make no money. They pay no taxes.
All they have to worry about are mine.*

EXTREMELY CREDIBLE:

Something I think I heard somewhere.

Trump-to-English Translator

TRUMP

"I could stand in the middle of Fifth Avenue
and shoot somebody, and I wouldn't lose voters."

–Rally in Sioux Center, Iowa

ENGLISH

No one supports guns more than I do.

Trump-to-English Translator

TRUMP

"After I beat them, I'm going to be so presidential, you're going to be so bored, you're going to say, this is the most boring human being I've ever interviewed."

–Fox News Sunday interview

ENGLISH

Come on. Be real. Does anyone want a boring Trump?
You want my TV ratings to go as low as unwatchable SNL?

If you talk about yourself in the third person, people think you're more objective.

Trump-to-English Translator

TRUMP

"Don't believe those phony numbers when you hear
4.9 and 5 percent unemployment. The number's probably 28, 29,
as high as 35. In fact, I even heard recently 42 percent."

–New Hampshire primary victory speech

ENGLISH

Don't believe any phony numbers until I am president.

Trump-to-English Translator

TRUMP

"Donald J. Trump is calling for a total and complete shutdown of Muslims entering the United States until our country's representatives can figure out what the hell is going on."

–Rally in South Carolina, December 7, 2015

ENGLISH

We are going to institute what I call "Not a Muslim ban."

Trump-to-English Translator

TRUMP

"ISIS is honoring President Obama. He is the founder of ISIS.
He is the founder of ISIS, OK? He's the founder.
He founded ISIS. And I would say the co-founder
would be crooked Hillary Clinton."

—RALLY IN SUNRISE, FLORIDA

ENGLISH

Obama is the reason for all bad things. Titanic?
Obama. Hindenburg? Obama. Katrina?
Obama with a little help from Hillary.

ALTERNATIVE FACT:

The lead article on Breitbart.com.

Trump-to-English Translator

TRUMP

"One thing I can promise you is this:
I will always tell you the truth."

–Rally in Charlotte, North Carolina

ENGLISH

Fake news! Sucker!

EVERYBODY GETS
A TRUMPITUDE NICKNAME

When someone treats you "not very nice," show who has
the Trumpitude. Assign another schoolyard nickname.
Some are instantly familiar. Isn't that right, "Pocahontas"?
You hear me, "Low Energy"? But who's "Wacky" and who's
"Truly Weird"? Try to match them all.

A.	1 for 38	1.	Barack Obama
B.	Baby	2.	Bernie Sanders
C.	Corrupt	3.	Chuck Schumer
D.	Crazy	4.	Elizabeth Warren
E.	Crooked	5.	Glenn Beck
F.	Cryin'	6.	Hillary Clinton
G.	Dumb as a Rock	7.	Jeb Bush
H.	Little	8.	Joe Biden
I.	Low Energy	9.	John Kasich
J.	Lyin'	10.	Marco Rubio
K.	Miss Piggy	11.	Mika Brzezinski
L.	Mr. Tough Guy	12.	Miss Universe Alicia Machado
M.	Pocahontas	13.	Rand Paul
N.	Truly Weird	14.	Ted Cruz
O.	Wacky	15.	Tim Kaine

EVERYBODY GETS
A TRUMPITUDE NICKNAME
CORRECT ANSWERS

A. 1 for 38
B. Baby
C. Corrupt
D. Crazy
E. Crooked
F. Cryin'
G. Dumb as a Rock
H. Little
I. Low Energy
J. Lyin'
K. Miss Piggy
L. Mr. Tough Guy
M. Pocahontas
N. Truly Weird
O. Wacky

9. John Kasich
1. Barack Obama
15. Tim Kaine
2. Bernie Sanders
6. Hillary Clinton
3. Chuck Schumer
11. Mika Brzezinski
10. Marco Rubio
7. Jeb Bush
14. Ted Cruz
12. Miss Universe Alicia Machado
8. Joe Biden
4. Elizabeth Warren
13. Rand Paul
5. Glenn Beck

Trump-to-English Translator

TRUMP

"This very expensive GLOBAL WARMING bullshit
has got to stop. Our planet is freezing."

–Tweet from @RealDonaldTrump

ENGLISH

How's a guy supposed to get a tan? #FakeTan

Trump-to-English Translator

TRUMP

"Happy #CincoDeMayo! The best taco bowls are made in Trump Tower Grill. I love Hispanics!"

—Tweet from @RealDonaldTrump

ENGLISH

I love Hispanics so much, I am going to deport their grandmothers and make their cousins pay for my big, beautiful wall. Adios, hombres!

Trump-to-English Translator

TRUMP

"This is more work than in my previous life."

—*Reuters* INTERVIEW

ENGLISH

Pretty please, can I stop being president now?

THE CLOSER:

One who swoops in noisily near the end and fails to make a deal.

Trump-to-English Translator

TRUMP

"I'm the king of debt. I understand debt better than probably anybody. I know how to deal with debt, so well. I love debt."

—CNN INTERVIEW

ENGLISH

Borrow money. Don't repay it. Now you too can be a very successful businessman. Or president.

ART OF THE DEAL:

A best-selling fantasy
novel from 1987.

Trump-to-English Translator

TRUMP

"It has not been easy for me. And you know I started off in Brooklyn. My father gave me a small loan of a million dollars."

—New Hampshire town hall

ENGLISH

My father taught me a lesson. He could have given me two million. Then, I could have made America twice as great.

Trump-to-English Translator

TRUMP

"You know the funny thing, I don't get along with rich people.
I get along with the middle class and the poor people
better than I get along with the rich people."

—ABC INTERVIEW ABOARD TRUMP FORCE ONE

ENGLISH

Being with poor people makes me feel rich.

GOP:

Abbreviation for Gushing Over Putin.

DRIVE WITH TRUMPITUDE

What? You expect Donald Trump to drive just any vehicle? Over the years, he's ended up behind the wheel of some mighty flashy rides...

Electric-blue Lamborghini Diablo
Mercedes-Maybach S600
Mercedes-Benz SLR McLaren
Cadillac Escalade
Gold Cadillac Allanté convertible
Rolls-Royce Silver Cloud
Rolls-Royce Phantom
Red Tesla Roadster
24-karat gold Orange County Chopper
2011 Chevy Camaro Indy 500 Pace Car
Black/gold E-Z-GO Freedom RXV Golf Cart

Presidential Cadillac One
Then there is the official vehicle the Secret Service won't let Trump drive. No car has more 'tude than Presidential Cadillac One. It comes equipped with Kevlar tires, pump-action shotguns, and tear gas cannons including one gun behind the front grille. The grille also has night-vision cameras. Only the driver's window opens and only 3 inches. All the windows are five layers thick. The doors are armor-plated and offer 100% protection from a chemical attack. The trunk is loaded with all kinds of medical goodies including bags of Rh-negative Trumpitude blood.

THE TRUTH:

TRUTH

An utterly irrelevant technicality.

TRUMP'S 24K
GOLDEN RULES

TRUMP'S 24K GOLDEN RULES

Two wrongs don't make a right...
    ...but they do make room for wife number 3.

Laugh as often and as loudly as possible...
    ...just not at the White House Correspondents' Dinner.

Actions speak louder than words...
    ...unless the words are "knock the crap out of them."

You can't judge a book by its cover...
    ...unless my face is on it, then buy it now.

Treat others as you wish to be
    treated...
    ...and demand that others
    treat you like you treat
    yourself.

Seize the day...
    ...and the oil in Iraq.

All that glitters is not gold...
    ...but gold always glitters—
    so why take a chance?

Put your best foot forward...
    ...as soon as you take it out
    of your mouth.

Age before beauty. Way before.

The early bird catches the
worm...
   ...and quickly tweets it
   out before anyone else
   is awake.

Keep your friends close....
   ...and the fake-news
   media closer.

Don't burn your bridges...
   ...unless you have a
   nonunion crew of
   undocumented workers
   standing by to rebuild
   them.

ME

Be your own worst enemy.

Treasure your friends...
   ...and choose friends with treasure.

As one door closes, another door opens...
   .... just be careful all those swinging doors don't hit you on the
   way out.

Manners cost nothing...
   .... having no manners costs nothing either.

Never be afraid to make a mistake....
   ...and surround yourself with staff to take the blame.

Worry only about things you can control...
    ...and make sure you control everything.

It's not what you know, it's who you know...
    ...and who you know that will lie about what you know.

Family comes first...
    ...when you're the first family.

SCRAMBLED TRUMP

Unscramble each of the Trump-favorite clue words.

ISPHC
◯ ☐ ◯ ☐

RSFIE
☐ ◯ ☐ ◯

GREBRU
☐ ☐ ◯ ☐ ◯◯

PHCEKTU
☐ ◯ ◯ ☐ ◯ ☐ ◯

TMAOFLEA
☐ ◯◯ ☐ ◯ ☐ ◯

NLDAMDSCO
☐ ◯◯ ☐ ☐ ◯◯◯ ☐ ◯

Your Answer:

Donald Trump's Marriage Policy

Take the circled letters and unscramble them for a special Trumpitude message.

❝◯◯◯◯◯◯◯ ◯◯◯ ◯◯◯◯◯◯◯◯❞

SCRAMBLED TRUMP

Unscramble each of the
Trump-favorite clue words.

Donald Trump's
Marriage Policy

ISPHC
C H I P S

RSFIE
F R I E S

GREBRU
B U R G E R

PHCEKTU
K E T C H U P

TMAOFLEA
M E A T L O A F

NLDAMDSCO
M C D O N A L D S

Your Answer:

Take the circled letters and
unscramble them for a
special Trumpitude
message.

"R E P E A L   A N D   R E P L A C E"

90

FINISH TRUMP'S
THOUGHT...

Finish Trump's Thought...

"Nobody knew health care could be so complicated..."

...Except for Hillary Clinton, Barack Obama, both parties in Congress, Big Pharma, Big Insurance, all patients, all nurses, all doctors including Dr. Phil, Dr. John, and Dr. Dre.

Finish Trump's Thought...

"Bing bing, bong bong bong, bing bing.
You know what that is, right?..."

...Don't worry, Putin understands the secret code.

No need to win before you declare
victory. Are you tired of winning yet?

Finish Trump's Thought...

"I think we've done more than perhaps any president in the first 100 days...."

...I played a lot of golf, got some me time at Mar-a-Lago, almost started a war with Australia and launched my 2020 campaign. Best of all, I fired Arnold Schwarzenegger.

Why hire incompetent strangers when you can hire incompetent family?

TRUMPITUDE SWEET NUTHINS'

He loves you, he loves you not. With Donald, sometimes it's hard to tell. Match these people with the actual words he's used about them.

A. Ben Carson

B. Bill Clinton

C. Chuck Todd

D. Dr. Jacob Bornstein

E. Hillary Clinton

F. Hillary Clinton

G. Ivanka Trump

H. James Comey

I. John Lewis

J. John McCain

K. Kim Jong-un

L. Lindsay Graham

M. Megyn Kelly

N. Melania Trump

O. Mitt Romney

P. Vladimir Putin

1. "A great doctor"

2. "All talk, no action"

3. "An okay doctor"

4. "Awkward and goofy"

5. "Bimbo"

6. "Dummy"

7. "Great senator"

8. "Great wife"

9. "A real nut job"

10. "Dumbest human being"

11. "She's got the best body"

12. "Sleepy eyes"

13. "Pretty smart cookie"

14. "Terrific in bed"

15. "Very smart"

16. "Wild Bill"

TRUMPITUDE SWEET NUTHINS' CORRECT ANSWERS

A. Ben Carson   3. "An okay doctor"
B. Bill Clinton   16. "Wild Bill"
C. Chuck Todd   12. "Sleepy eyes"
D. Dr. Jacob Bornstein   1. "A great doctor"
E. Hillary Clinton   7. "Great senator"
F. Hillary Clinton   8. "Great wife"
G. Ivanka Trump   11. "She's got the best body"
H. James Comey   9. "A real nut job"
I. John Lewis   2. "All talk, no action"
J. John McCain   6. "Dummy"
K. Kim Jong-un   13. "Pretty smart cookie"
L. Lindsay Graham   4. "Awkward and goofy"
M. Megyn Kelly   5. "Bimbo"
N. Melania Trump   14. "Terrific in bed"
O. Mitt Romney   10. "Dumbest human being"
P. Vladimir Putin   15. "Very smart"

Finish Trump's Thought...

"I've been against the war in Iraq from the beginning..."

...Which is why I kept telling Sean Hannity and Howard Stern and other people I was for the war. Because I was against it. From the beginning. I just didn't tell anyone.

Hire all the best people and don't let
them do their jobs.

Finish Trump's Thought...

"We will build a great wall along the southern border.
And Mexico will pay for the wall. One hundred percent.
They don't know it yet, but they're going to pay for it..."

*...Unless they say "no." Then maybe we'll just build
a big, beautiful fence. Or put up a sign that says,
"Por favor, no entrar. No bad hombres."*

Finish Trump's Thought...

"I believe in clean air. Immaculate air..."

...You should breathe the air in my sealed Trump Tower penthouse. Clean, immaculate. Except for my hairspray, which isn't made as good as it used to be and is definitely not damaging the ozone.

Finish Trump's Thought...

"We've got to be nice and cool, nice and calm.
All right, stay on point, Donald. Stay on point.
No sidetracks, Donald. Nice and easy..."

*...Last thing I remember was Melania slowly swinging a watch
and telling me to act more like a president—of a country!*

Russia good, China bad. Wait, reverse
that! No, reverse it again.

Finish Trump's Thought...

"I thought being president would be easier
than my old life..."

*...Do you know how hard it is letting people pay you
millions of dollars to put your name on things?*

Finish Trump's Thought...

"I think I am actually humble.
I think I'm much more humble than you would understand..."

...And I understand humble, believe me.
It means best bragger, right?

Loyalty is like 5th Avenue. It's a one-way street.

SUPER TRUMPITUDE

Some presidents are more SUPER than others, but only one president is truly SUPERlative! Who says Donald Trump has nothing to brag about?

–OLDEST elected president in U.S. history
–MOST brides before being elected
–MOST divorces of any president
–MOST books bearing his byline (whether he actually wrote them or not)
–LONGEST ties of any president
–MOST television reality programs starred in
–MOST golf courses owned
–MOST holes of golf played
–MOST tweets of any President...and 2nd MOST followers of any president on Twitter (58 million fewer than President Obama)
–MOST self-named buildings
–LEAST number of pets in the White House in over 100 years—— ZERO pooches or pussies
–MOST inexperienced—politically and militarily
–MOST GOP Primary votes for and the MOST GOP Primary votes against
–Knows the "BEST words"—Donald Trump in South Carolina
–"HEALTHIEST individual ever elected president," according to personal physician Dr. Harold Bornstein

Finish Trump's Thought...

"I know more about ISIS than the generals do.
Believe me..."

*...Generally speaking, just not when it comes to details,
ideas, plans, facts, combat operations...*

Surround yourself with all the best people, then cut 'em off at the knees.

Finish Trump's Thought...

"All the dress shops are sold out in Washington.
It's hard to find a great dress for this inauguration..."

...But if all the pretty ladies want to come naked...

Finish Trump's Thought...

"I'm speaking with myself, number one, because I have a very good brain, and I've said a lot of things..."

... And, number two, because Melania stopped listening years ago.

RAP WITH TRUMPITUDE

Rappers love rapping about Trump, and not always flatteringly. Match the artist and song with its Trumpitude Shout-Out.

1. "Johnny Ryall" by Beastie Boys
2. "I Gotta Say What Up!!!" by Ice Cube
3. "What More Can I Say" by Jay-Z
4. "Three Strikes You In" by Ice Cube
5. "Shut Up Bitch" by Lil Kim
6. "Paid" by Kid Rock
7. "Hip Hop Quotables" by Ludacris
8. "Mo Cars, Mo Hoes" by Fabolous
9. "Mafioso" by Kool G Rap
10. "So Appalled" by Kanye West
11. "I Need Dollas" by T.I.
12. "Money and the Power" by Scarface
13. "Da Funk" by Redman
14. "211" by Master P
15. "Black Friday" by Kendrick Lamar

A. At the Trump International
B. Balding Donald Trump
C. More cash than Trump
D. Donald Tramp
E. I'm thinking Donald Trump
F. I'm Trump of the pumpers
G. In the Trump International
H. In Trump Plaza
I. Makin' more than Donald Trump
J. Meetings with Donald Trump
K. Paid like Trump
L. Rich like Trump
M. Stackin' paper like Trump
N. Voting for Donald Trump
O. Well known like Donald Trump

RAP WITH TRUMPITUDE
CORRECT ANSWERS

1. "Johnny Ryall" by Beastie Boys
2. "I Gotta Say What Up!!!" by Ice Cube
3. "What More Can I Say" by Jay-Z
4. "Three Strikes You In" by Ice Cube
5. "Shut Up Bitch" by Lil Kim
6. "Paid" by Kid Rock
7. "Hip Hop Quotables" by Ludacris
8. "Mo Cars, Mo Hoes" by Fabolous
9. "Mafioso" by Kool G Rap
10. "So Appalled" by Kanye West
11. "I Need Dollas" by T.I.
12. "Money and the Power" by Scarface
13. "Da Funk" by Redman
14. "211" by Master P
15. "Black Friday" by Kendrick Lamar

D. Donald Tramp
I. Makin' more than Donald Trump
A. At the Trump International
L. Rich like Trump
G. In the Trump International
K. Paid like Trump
J. Meetings with Donald Trump
F. I'm Trump of the pumpers
H. In Trump plaza
B. Balding Donald Trump
E. I'm thinking Donald Trump
M. Stackin' paper like Trump
O. Well known like Donald Trump
C. More cash than Trump
N. Voting for Donald Trump

Finish Trump's Thought...

"I would bring back waterboarding. And I'd bring back
a hell of a lot worse than waterboarding..."

...I'll make the terrorists watch endless Gary Busey movies.
They'll beg for the beautiful waterboard.

But I don't want you in our nuclear club.

Finish Trump's Thought...

"Don't worry, I'll give it up after I'm president.
We won't tweet anymore, I don't think.
Not presidential..."

*...I'll stop tweeting just as soon as I stop holding rallies,
stop smooching Putin, stop bashing my critics,
and stop hiring my kids.*

They can cut off my fingers
and cut off my toes—I'm not worried.
I'll tweet with my nose.

Finish Trump's Thought...

"Look at my African-American here!..."

...He's right by the colored guy.

Finish Trump's Thought...

"And by the way, just so you know,
I am the least racist person, the least racist person
that you've ever seen, the least..."

*... I am announcing my utter lack of racism
in the capital of the old Confederacy.*

Finish Trump's Thought...

"I feel like a supermodel except, like, times 10, OK?
It's true. I'm a supermodel..."

*... My hair, my figure, my extra-long ties—this season,
I'm coming back in style.*

Never take bald for an answer.

Finish Trump's Thought...

"I watched when the World Trade Center came tumbling down.
And I watched in Jersey City, N.J., where thousands
and thousands of people were cheering as that building was
coming down. Thousands of people were cheering..."

*...What do you mean thousands of people weren't cheering?
No one cheered? Really? Then, never mind.
But I still say they cheered.*

Finish Trump's Thought...

"Sorry losers and haters, but my I.Q. is one of the highest—
and you all know it! Please don't feel so stupid or insecure,
it's not your fault..."

*...I just say all this dumb stuff to make you feel better about yourself.
#MakeAmericaUneducatedAgain*

Ignore all leaks ... unless you hear
them directly from me.

Finish Trump's Thought...

"My fingers are long and beautiful, as, it has been well documented, are various other parts of my body..."

... I've measured. And in millimeters, I'm huuuuuge.

Finish Trump's Thought...

"I'm a very big person when it comes to the environment.
I have received awards on the environment..."

*... And every time I need room for more exciting awards,
I drop the environment ones in the RECYCLE bin.*

Finish Trump's Thought...

"I'll take jobs back from China, I'll take jobs back from Japan.
The Hispanics are going to get those jobs,
and they're going to love Trump..."

*... And just when they get comfortable,
I'll deport them.*

Every bully pulpit needs a bully.

Finish Trump's Thought...

"I would not be a president who took vacations.
I would not be a president that takes time off..."

*...Just remember, leaving the White House to stay at any of my
many, many properties—some of the best buildings in the world—
that doesn't count. And golf? Not time off. None of that counts.*

SEARCHING FOR THE BEST TRUMPITUDE WORDS

```
S I W R A I D E M T S E N O H S I D J Y
L Y L R I A F N U R T N U H H C T I W E
Y A U O V E R R A T E D O N J R H V H P
N E P N A S T Y W O M A N H R H G E C O
A T E M Y S S A L C G G A Y E U U R I D
F O I E A Q B T N N M T N C I G O Y R Y
F T B O N W J A O U E U A O H E T G Y L
I A G I O A S R D R T R S A R B W O L G
T L N L T I W E S D G A E L O R D O L I
H D I E N N O G H S U L E J I E A D A B
G I N A I A V B I T P D T R Z M S B E F
N S N K C L S D L O N U E X G H B R R A
I A I E E E B O E U N I T S W C K A J K
R S W R D M S P E C B R A A O E Y I N E
O T A U U E F I V A N K A R P G A N R N
B E A D R O A C O V F E F E D P K K I E
V R P P S B E A U T I F U L W A L L G W
F S F T C I R E E M E V E I L E B Z F S
O L O W R A T I N G S T E R R I B L E K
W L B I L L I O N S N O T A P U P P E T
```

SAD	DOPEY	HATERS	BILLIONS	REALLY RICH
DUMB	DON JR	IVANKA	DISGRACE	LOTS OF PEOPLE
ERIC	FRAUD	LEAKER	FAKE NEWS	BEAUTIFUL WALL
HUGE	GREAT	NUTJOB	TERRIBLE	DRAIN THE
LOW RATINGS	LOSER	COVFEFE	UNFAIRLY	SWAMP
MUSLIM BAN	TOUGH	MELANIA	BELIEVE ME	TOTAL DISASTER
NASTY WOMAN	WRONG	NOT NICE	MUSLIM BAN	VERY GOOD
TAPP	BARRON	TIFFANY	OVERRATED	BRAIN
WEAK	BORING	WINNING	WITCH HUNT	DISHONEST
BIGLY	CLASSY	BAD DUDES	NOT A PUPPET	MEDIA

SEARCHING FOR THE BEST
TRUMPITUDE WORDS
ANSWER KEY

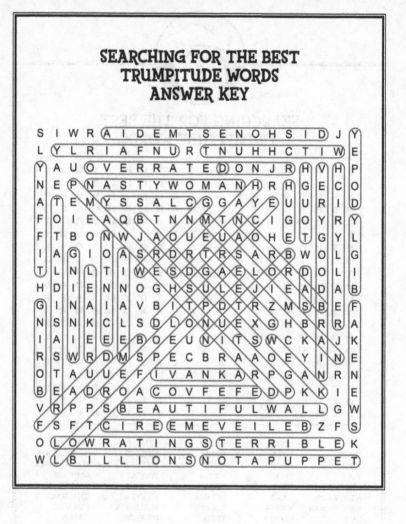

Finish Trump's Thought...

"I know a lot of bad people in this country that are making a hell of a lot of money and not paying taxes..."

...And one good person who is making a hell of a lot of money and not paying taxes. Hello!

Demand steak with ketchup wherever you travel. Eating foreign food is leading from behind.

Finish Trump's Thought...

"I'm a believer in the polls, by the way.
Rarely do you see a poll that's very far off..."

*...Except for approval ratings after you get elected.
Lies. Fake news. Those are total frauds.*

The buck stops, oh, pretty much anywhere.

Finish Trump's Thought...

"And we've had leaders like Susan B. Anthony—
have you heard of Susan B. Anthony?
I'm shocked that you've heard of her..."

...She was on a coin. Who carries coins?

Finish Trump's Thought...

"I will absolutely apologize sometime in the hopefully distant future if I'm ever wrong..."

...Maybe after I'm dead. If then.

I don't want to be president anymore!
Being president is hard!!!

ACKNOWLEDGEMENTS

Thanks to artist Randy Jones for taking this patriotic journey with boundless enthusiasm and twisted genius, and to his talented wife, Susann Jones, for being a perfect coconspirator.

Thanks to Anthony Ziccardi and Billie Brownell at Post Hill Press and to Peter McGuigan and Claire Harris at Foundry Literary + Media—and to attorney James Gregorio—for making the publishing process far more fun than it ought to be.

Thanks to my Metro editors, Gary Kane, Jason Nuckolls, Morgan Rousseau, and Alek Korab, for seeing Trump's America as the rich landscape that it is.

A special thank you to Roberta Teer for her creative input, organizational prowess and, from her school-district days, first-string puzzle-crafting skills.

I'd be nowhere without you all.

ABOUT THE AUTHORS

Ellis Henican is a journalist and bestselling author. As a
columnist for *New York Newsday* and the *Metro* papers, he has
spent far too long staring into Donald Trump's shifty eyes.
Henican's commentaries on Trump and other topics are featured
often on CNN, MSNBC, and Fox News. His website is henican.com.

Randy Jones is an artist and illustrator whose satirical work has
appeared in *The New York Times*, *The Wall Street Journal*, *National
Lampoon*, *Playboy*, and many other media outlets, fake and
otherwise. His website is randyjonesart.com.